I follow in the dust she raises

I follow
in the dust she raises

Linda Martin

University of Alaska Press
Fairbanks

© 2015 University of Alaska Press
All rights reserved

University of Alaska Press
P.O. Box 756240
Fairbanks, AK 99775-6240

ISBN 978-1-60223-255-6 (paperback); ISBN 978-1-60223-256-3 (electronic)

Library of Congress Cataloging-in-Publication Data

Martin, Linda, 1945–
  [Poems. Selections]
  I follow in the dust she raises / Linda Martin.
      pages cm
  ISBN 978-1-60223-255-6 (paperback : acid-free paper)—ISBN 978-1-60223-256-3 (electronic)
  I. Title.
  PS3613.A7827A6 2015
  811'.6—dc23
                        2014023207
Cover art: *Winged Grace* by Janice Peyton
Cover design by Jen Gunderson
Interior Design by Natalie Taylor

This publication was printed on acid-free paper that meets the minimum requirements for ANSI / NISO Z39.48–1992 (R2002) (Permanence of Paper for Printed Library Materials).

For my mother, Ida Katherine Harbine, who wanted the best for me—and for Larry, who is the best.

contents

IV. Contemplating Autumn

I. running through shadows

visiting the cemetery in plains, montana

From here the rocky ridge marking the farm
slants downriver like a pasture gate standing open.

Cheatgrass and knapweed tangle the graveyard edge.
Grazing mule deer flick long ears in my direction.

In the town below, prosperity has come and gone:
granary turned to gift shop, sawmill shut down.

At my feet, the names of brother, father, mother—
three granite stories I read again and again.

mythology

The day my father died, tamarack flared school-bus yellow
on the dark hills. Frozen clods in the plowed field pushed
hard against my shoes. The grownups spoke of heaven.
Not gone, I heard them say, just traveling someplace far away.

I carry his absence the way he carried his Homelite chainsaw,
leaning away from its weight for balance. Somewhere he sails
the South Pacific, wraps himself in tapa cloth, rides like a gaucho
over the pampas. Mama feeds the legend with her stories.

Living lonely in Manhattan, I dream him into life.
He shows up on East Fiftieth, numinous and tan, blue shirt
rough to the touch, smelling of tobacco. I wake bereft.
He has turned up his jacket collar, put on his hat and left.

a sumptuous destitution

Nothing but mourning dove and willow tree,
mountains throwing shadow.
Rope taps on a graveyard flagpole—
loud in granite silence.

Colors weave through dark wool,
chainsaw oil spills on dusty canvas.
Drumming grouse, bugling elk, coyote song.
Beneath each tamarack, a golden needlepoint.

In winter clouds, a sudden flare like burnished wings.
Snowshoe hare keeps still as root under the spruce.
Strong current on an outgoing tide pulls me far from shore,
as the sun sets and a full moon rises.

Each loss a sweeping away, and then,
like a tidal change, a lavish fullness.
Death, an end to the world, the world going on.

believers

1.

Mama visits women made plain by faith.
Hair in buns, no color, no fun,
wedding bands their sole adornment.
Holier-than-thou
she calls them, straightening
her proud shoulders, smoothing
her purple Guatemalan skirt.

At Eastertime my little brother
crouches in a low kitchen cupboard,
producing egg after sugary egg
like a magic chicken. He is as surprised
as I am. Our parents and their friends
weep with laughter, some playful
presence embracing us all.

2.

Mama talks to the priest
about the soul of our oldest brother,
sixteen years old when a hunter shot him.
No baptism, no heaven, so Mama
breaks ties with Rome, her heart wounded,
her mind open to any hopeful doctrine.

When buttercups finally bloom,
shining yellow next to the barn,
religion and doubt melt like snowbanks.
I hunt dime-sized flowers as if color
were a child's proof of resurrection.
Each blossom makes Mama clap her hands.

running through shadows

1.

June 1952. *On your mark.* We're hands and feet in warm dust, barefoot so he can check our tracks for that straight stride he preaches. No pigeon-toes. No toeing out. *Get set.* We imitate track stars, crouching, eyes straight ahead, small eager coils ready to run. *Go.* We're off, Chic and I, arms and legs pumping, racing between alfalfa fields to the fence line, a hard right and uphill to the pole gate. We touch the poles, whirl back toward our coach, our timekeeper, our laughing father. Meadowlarks sing.

2.

October 1945. Our parents call him Twinks, because he twinkles. I see him in black and white. A lock of dark hair falls over his forehead as he stands arm in arm with his two best friends. He holds the state high school record for the mile run. In a forest near our farm a hunter with buck fever mistakes him for a deer. Our parents give Chic our brother's name, just as it reads on the tombstone.

3.

April 1929. The crash is coming. He takes his mark with two hundred others in New York City. Will Rogers fires the starting gun. Our father runs to Los Angeles, seventy-eight days away, where our mother waits with our sister and the brother we never knew. Newsmen name the race Bunion Derby, follow our father across the country telling of rain and mud, sun and dust, preposterous effort. He finishes in the money, prize never paid.

dancing with mama

Mama sways on tiptoe with a long-handled saw
to prune the forest, bends from the waist
to pick huckleberries,
waltzes a rattlesnake dead with a hoe.

A wave of her apron sends the bull to the pen.
Like Martha Graham dancing *Lamentation*
costumed in a dishtowel mask,
Mama stirs fungicide into the wheat seed.

High kicks as she cleans the house.
We call the cows at milking time,
the pasture gate a ballet barre.
I learn first position, plié.

Mama swears in motion—*damnation.*
Stamps foot, hands on hips.
Hell's bells. Turns on her heel.
I follow in the dust she raises.

a visit from aunt rosie

Mama's sister Rosie stands child-sized.
Her voice sounds raspy and sweet.
When she plays with my brother and me
the farm doesn't feel so lonesome.

Mama takes us aside. *Dear ones,* she says.

We help Rosie duck through fences. She knows
new games, laughs at our grade-school jokes.
Rosie sits on a backless bench Mama built for her,
wears dresses Mama sews to cover her hump of spine.

When someone looks different—

We're proud to take Aunt Rosie to town,
but people stare and stare.

We should all be kind enough not to notice.

logger song

*I know you are a logger
and not just a common bum...*
　　　　　—from a song my father sang

Rich pitch of pine, sweet tobacco.
Hidden grouse drumming.

Buck walks the length of a log.
His saw croons and rumbles, branches fall.

Sun slants on sumac and Oregon grape.
Through the woods a tenor voice calls

TIMBER! A hesitation, green wood cracks,
a long airy fall, a long solid whomp.

Then Charlie hollers:
Let's put on the feed bag.

Black tin boxes, peanut butter,
deviled ham, oranges.

Toothless Niemi files the chain on his Homelite.
Buck plays "Clementine" on harmonica.

Resting on forest duff, they pass the thermos,
hum a song about coffee stirred with a thumb.

widowmaker

Dad builds a canny camp trailer
out of plywood and tarpaper,
prow-fronted like a boat.
In the bow, a woodstove,
storage for his chainsaw.
He puts his bed on hinges, nails
leather loops for kitchen tools,
then hauls his wheeled house
to logging jobs in the woods.

Back home, Mama keeps
cows milked, pasture gates closed.
Sometimes she warns me—*Don't
marry a man who works away.*

Our Holstein bloats on alfalfa,
Mama meets a bobcat in the chicken coop,
the pump loses its prime. Some afternoons I sit
on the riverbank with Mama, learning to worry.

On a job up the Lochsa River
Dad works alone and late,
bucking logs pushed over
by a D-6 dozer.
He revs his Homelite
one last time,
cuts through a leaning hemlock,
close to the butt of the tree.

a young child

—after G. M. H.

All my thoughts are fresh.
Buttercups, imagined friends,
fresh raspberries with fresh cream.
I cry for storybook horses,
Tornado Boy lost and hungry.
Of real grief I have
a brother's name on granite,
my mother's tears, her affinity
for weeping willow and mourning dove.
When my father dies, I'm in a story.
I weep without knowing why,
take the role of orphan girl
playing a fanciful sorrow.
Fakery spreads its secret blight
over my wan, wounded heart.

pearly everlasting

Mama grieves among the pines
with a Swede saw and a pruner,
grooming her far-field woodland,
making glades for buttercups,
stacking brush for burning.

She dresses clean and bright,
making an effort. Won't let
herself go, the way a widow might.
Sometimes she sings Irish love songs,
or stands still and remembers.

Mama walks home along the river,
planning tamale pie for dinner.
From the forest she carries *immortalis*—
tiny, white papery flowers that will last
when she takes them to the graves.

II. history lesson

watching mama's figure

Ample, Mama called her bosom,
and it was. Soft like bread, and warm.
When she called the cows and they lumbered
across the pasture, udders swaying
heavily beneath them,
Mama wrapped both arms
across her troublesome breasts,
danced high kicks to stir her blood.
Shoulders back, she'd tell me,
correcting her posture as she spoke.
Proud and voluptuous as royalty
we strolled through fields of wheat and alfalfa.
You're pretty, a friend of my father said,
but you can't hold a candle to your mother.
He had one eye on Mama's figure,
the other on a widow's farmland.

older sister

When I sport a short haircut,
I think of my sister, Ruth.
Never let your ears show,
she told me once, pulling
my thick braids back.
A raving beauty with stern ideas,
Ruthie collected marriage proposals
as if they were dance corsages.
Her posture was even straighter
than Mama's. My birth
embarrassed her. She thought
Mama was getting fat.

Ruthie and Mama discussed things
that weren't for me to hear.
During family visits I sat
at the low table with Ruthie's children,
eavesdropping like mad on womanly
conversation. My ears were good for that.

uppity

When the Angus bull lifts his big black head
and bellows into the night, Mama describes
San Francisco foghorns.
Coyotes howl from cliffs across the river
as she teaches me to walk with a book on my head,
studying perfect posture.
Tractor dust, crankcase oil, cow manure,
bath water heated on the woodstove.
Mama sews my ruffled dresses, brushes my hair
one hundred strokes. I get chilblains from wearing
patent leather Mary Janes.

The clerks at the Mercantile
know we're country. I see them judging
Mama's efforts, her high heels,
her good tweed. She's out of fashion.
I begin to want the right accessories,
the store-bought confidence of a city girl.

I leave the farm. Professors teach me
to abhor innocence, mistrust nature,
rise above weather.
I wear education like a velvet cape,
swirling knowledge around my country self,
until I'm better than Mama. She applauds
my arrogance. Like poor posture,
too much humility cripples a woman.

refusing a man

Rick stands on the library steps
wearing his ROTC dress uniform.
The olive-green jacket nips in at his waist,
creased trousers break perfectly over
the lowest laces of his polished boots.
Under the military hat with its stiff short bill,
his pained expression has authority.
History falls over us. I'm in love
with the Renaissance; he has a foot
in Vietnam. With one last look
he judges my future, lacking him.
I feel like a guilty child
but I'm twenty-one, as old as he.
Clutching books to my chest,
confused, I turn away—free.

moonwalking, 1969

One year into my shaky first marriage,
astronauts land on the moon.
I walk through forest windfall
where the downed trees are old, silvery,
scrambled like sticks in a child's game.
I pick a route over, around. The moon
shows silverwhite in a noon sky.
I look up, a moonstruck woman.
For one sweet minute
it's just Armstrong and me,
stepping into difficult terrain.

losing a man

He hooks his rough-out leather jacket
over his shoulder with one finger,
like Redford. Money worries
annoy him, the same as gnats
at a yacht club picnic.
He drives us home by the hill road,
cornering turns like Andretti.
He parks the Porsche underground
at the apartment we can't afford.

Since it's the seventies
he lights a Marlboro,
squints at me through smoke,
like Bukowski. I am full of scorn,
but then he says: *Not cute anymore.*
Not fun. The pain surprises me.
It lasts for years.

city girl

At first I walked to work through Grand Central Station,
casting clear-eyed glances right and left. Here I am,
New York, New York. Nice-looking people looked
askance. Gray-suited men, women in lovely coats,
everyone in a hurry, avoiding me.

In time I learned to walk like I knew
where I was going. I could look
right through a man, hold sympathy at bay.

I could eat eggplant parmesan at a diner on Kensington,
ignoring hungry, homeless people as they gazed
through the window at my plate.

history lesson

I played a blue-eyed Sacajawea—long braids and a farmgirl tan—
rode my buckskin bareback, crept through lodgepole thickets,
caught squawfish in the Clark Fork River.

In grade school I loved a shiny-haired Salish boy
named Delbert Dupuis. He lived in town so he knew
how to buy candy at the store, how to play marbles for keeps.
He pushed the merry-go-round for me.

Delbert moved away one summer. I didn't look up
from books, from my childish practice of sorrow to notice.
Twenty years later he died, after a fight at the Evaro Bar,
after a stint in Vietnam, after alcohol blurred him.

I remember him this way: On the first day of school in 1952,
in a room with more children than I'd seen in my life,
Delbert took my hand.

pigeons in montpelier

Say you grew up out west. Half a century ago, you had a fourth-grader's handle on important facts, understood how history happened east of you. So when you take the Montpelier exit off Interstate 80, catch sight of a golden capitol dome, you know Vermont: maple syrup, granite, Green Mountain Boys. You don't know the failure of the clothespin factory, the disastrous overpayment of a contractor, but you guess the only gold leaf in this town covers the capitol; the only thrill, the Winooski River running high. On this winter day, mountain backdrop gray, stone spires on every church, library lasting beyond a century, Montpelier seems remarkable for the rainbow shades of pigeons parading each historical ledge, strutting with contemporary confidence, possessing the city like a flock of western fourth-graders.

anonymous

Alone in a motel room in Sandpoint, Idaho,
she approves what she sees in the mirror:
A woman of average size, dressed in neutral colors,
with—at present—no particular function.

In the parking lot, a rental car. In her purse,
a plane ticket, a credit card, a little cash.

Behind her, mother and brothers visited.
Up ahead, husband and children waiting;
also the job, the house, the bills.

But tonight she is neither here nor there,
alone, a shadow behind the window shade.

The thought comes, solid as the bedside table with its Gideon Bible:
How pleasing to exist in the world, without being of it.

mama calls herself weary

Mama puts the tractor in the river.
She burns the bottom of every pan,
drives the wrong way on a highway exit.

Mama drags her feet. She frowns.
She falls like a tree in the strawberry patch,
and cannot rise without my help.

She sits in a blue wingback chair
tilting to her left, a flowered scarf
drooping across her rounded shoulders.

To look at her now, I could forget
how she danced a dusty ballet
on her way to milk the cows.

mama's will

We gather on Mama's ninetieth birthday,
supplicants spread across her living room
like a quilt. Parkinson's disease
shows on her face as sorrow,
like the Irish melancholy she expunged
with dance when she could dance,
or sang away in the golden days
when she drove her Allis-Chalmers tractor
across a fallow field beside a turquoise river.

Grandchildren, great-grandchildren,
a son who drinks, a son who bends the law,
two moody daughters, the unfaithful
daughter-in-law Mama adores—all together
for Mama's sake. In the face of our imperfections
she dotes on us, smiling against disease,
willing us to love each other.

At the nursing home a few weeks later,
Mama has a surge of energy—enough
to dance in place as she holds onto a chair,
enough to return to her narrow bed,
to the wall of family portraits beside it
where she admires our beauty once more.
Then she lies down to sleep.

the vanished

On the Clark Fork River in a rented boat,
I'm floating past the home place.
Can't help noticing how brave I look,
alone on the water, escorted
by arrows of geese pointing west.

I rode a buckskin mare along this river,
the horse a deal Mama struck
when she caught a neighbor, Tex,
taking hay bales from her barn.

Steering to shore, I read *No Trespassing,*
posted by the current owner, son
of the neighbor who left a calf fetus
on our porch after my father died,
to spook the fence-building widow.

When my brother plowed this field,
stone tools turned up—grooved, smooth,
shaped by hands like ours. Mama
held those stones with reverence,
admiring the vanished.

III. after years

at home now in homer

Say your life reforms itself and brings you here, to this spruce-and-alder town beside a changeable sea. Thirty years pass, changing familiar things so slowly you hardly remember gravel on Main Street, a library too small for its books. You learn to love boats, to can salmon. The downtown junkyard becomes a park, your children grow up and leave home, the economy fluctuates with the price of fish and oil. Restaurants change hands, banks change names, volcanoes across the inlet belch steam and ash. The red-leaf rose you planted years ago spreads down the creek bank below your dining room window. Each spring the varied thrush sends his note ringing through the trees in your backyard.

after years of searching

Larry is sleeping.
Ida and Tad are sleeping.
I set out three Easter baskets
next to the pot of yellow chrysanthemums
Larry brought home to me last night.
Nesting magpies squawk in the spruce.
I have seen them flying with twigs
long enough to put them off balance.
I hear the long note of a varied thrush.
If Mama could speak to me now she'd say
This is what I wanted you to have.

artifacts

If my daughter asks
about the man before her father,
I might confess to keeping a box of pictures
on the top shelf of the sewing cabinet
under these quilting scraps.

Here he is beside the green Chevy,
this is me with an ice axe on Mount Rainier.
There you see the two of us
in matching ski sweaters.

In the kitchen I could dig up
an eggbeater, a rolling pin,
several plates in a pattern
I no longer care for. As for

the wedding ring, I dropped it
into the silverware drawer
when I left, taking exactly
half of the stainless.

once upon a time

When frogs talked to fairies,
and balloons had conversations,
rhubarb leaves were dress-up hats
for my green-eyed girl.

She walked through the garden
with her elderberry wand,
wondering which flowers might marry.

I had vegetables to harvest,
a man to please, a kitchen floor
that needed wax.

I should have told her a story about Sweet
William and Alyssum. I could have
taken off my canvas gloves
to help her make a starflower bouquet.

During the ceremony I'm sure
the golden-crowned sparrow
would have been pleased to sing
the wistful way he's singing now.

building a boat

Father and daughter set out to build
a plywood boat of fourteen feet.

Forward and back with sanding blocks
they move together through her fourteenth year,

singing along to radio oldies,
under halogen spotlights in the shop.

She knows all the words to "Wild Thing."
He teaches her how to run a drill.

It takes four hands to hold things in place
as they stitch plank to plank with wire and glue.

Transom, breasthook, gunwales, thwarts—
the boat takes on a floatable shape.

Like scientists behind white masks
they lay down glass and epoxy.

Then the paint in her shade of blue,
in three slow, careful coats.

Time to place the oarlocks,
wrap leather at the pivot points,

fasten a line to the graceful bow,
truck the boat to the harbor.

He kneels on the dock and shoves her off.
Forward and back she bends to the oars.

He watches from shore as she rows away,
her boat like a leaf on the water.

boy, still visible

Nine of his baseball caps
hang on my wall like a quilt.

I've patched the ceiling upstairs
where he drilled holes to hang his bed.

The rusty gas tank from his first Subaru
rests against the woodshed like a breastplate.

That roof collapsing on his spruce-log fort
resembles my old authority over his life.

without fame

The hug puts my bifocals askew, my ear
against his heart as if this were an Apgar test.
His teeth white and straight, his muscles solid,
he's taller than I remember.

A year and a half since he's been home—
even as we touch he's headed farther north.
He tells me of his house and dog, his job,
smiles as he speaks of a woman in his life.

A mother is without fame, a pause in the journey.
Like Odysseus passing through town, my son
lifts two red duffels from the baggage carousel.

shopping for satisfaction

I'd be driving through Manhattan
with cash in my pocket, headed
for the designer clothing section
of Bloomingdale's department store.
Sometimes Mama was in the dream with me,
clutching the dashboard, her face lit up
with shopping zeal.

I could smell the store in my sleep—rose-scented air,
fine cloth. I heard the murmur of well-coiffed clerks,
the shuffle of money. Before I could get there,
before I could possess the maroon cable-knit sweater,
the sleek, pleated, soft wool slacks that fit like a dream—
I'd wake up.

Again and again this guilty, greedy
dream, until I paid three hundred dollars
for a raw-silk, fully lined Austin Reed dress
from Barrie Pace and wore it to a family wedding
where I upstaged my former sister-in-law,
the fashionable mother of the bride.

That dress was Mama's shade of aqua.
The double-breasted style, the oyster-shell buttons
were favorites of hers. She would have adored
the long matching chiffon scarf. She would have
approved the occasion, the costly spite.

true minds

When the doctor told me cancer,
you held my hand and couldn't talk.
I have always wanted words,
but I loved your mute devotion:
the way you brought four pillows
when I asked for one.

marriage vow

Drugs begin to fuzz the facts.
I feel the cozy breast of the nurse
who leans to tap my veins.
The anesthesiologist
in his green scrubs, his gauzy white cap,
resembles a dandelion gone to seed.
The gurney wheels start to move.
You smile as if we needn't worry,
looking like you did on Jackson Street
when you turned around on your motorcycle,
declared your love for me.

migrations

Here in Alaska crows congregate,
hold public meetings on the roofline
of Wells Fargo Bank.
From Louisiana our daughter reports
a whiskered school of catfish in the bayou.
Hundreds, Mom, all sizes.
Our son photographs an antelope herd
in northern Montana. *Like Africa,* he says,
amazed by numbers. Meanwhile, you and I
check the weather in three different time zones,
recall for one another how our girl sang
"Wild Thing," how our boy built a bed
and hung it from the ceiling
in this quiet house.

proof of joy

Sun through the bay window at two in the afternoon
on the shortest day of the year.

Scores of small birds at the feeder.
A child waves, wearing mittens I gave her.

Skis waxed to kick, glide. Eagles above me
like banners. Breath frosts my eyelashes.

In the kitchen—potato, carrot, bay leaf, onion.
On the sewing table, material for a woolen jacket.

Snow-covered roof, woodbox full, your
red Chevy work truck clattering into the yard.

IV. contemplating autumn

anniversary

When there were children in this house I longed
to be alone with you. Now, here we are.

She's married, pregnant.
He's working, driving a new pickup.

Once our little boy pointed at a lake.
See that flaming of blue?
Our baby girl watched a cat
traverse a fallen tree.
Catalog, she said.

premonition

The thin priest in the hospital elevator
seems overwhelmed by vestments,
by holy books, by sacrament.
The need for grace frightens me.
I turn my face.

the system

She walks both dogs by herself,
doesn't want them to get loose.

She fusses in the kitchen,
stacking dishes, soaking pans,
refusing help from anyone.

She calls the coroner, the insurance agent,
talks to the doctor and the mortician.
Seriously, she says. *Seriously.*

She folds the baby clothes,
stores them in a U-Haul box.
She has a system of her own.

september clouds

...for Zoey

Yellow kayak nudges a silver shoreline,
three cellophaned bouquets bungeed to the bow.
I slip into my spray skirt, zip up my life vest.

Kayak swings like a compass needle on the bay, east
toward Halibut Cove, south to Haystack Rock.
High September clouds, waves like folds in a comforter.

Grieving my daughter's infant daughter, I paddle west,
unwrap her birthday roses, set them lavishly adrift.
Mountains curve toward the open sea.

One tiny feather skims lightly on the tide, white,
fine as baby hair, beside me a moment and gone.

ordinary dangers

Heavy rain and more traffic than I'm used to. I smile
at one man and scrape the truck fender of another.

Ladder, roof, chimney brush. Like a spoon
in the blender, an impulse toward mishap.

You recover from breaking both heels,
I drop a glass bowl, forget to turn off the oven.

You bump your head on the bird feeder.
I survive two bouts of cancer.

Those nights when you're out of town,
unmoored dread vibrates through dark rooms—

the sound of one heart pounding.
Soon enough, one of us will lose the other.

acting my age

There's a liver spot on my right hand.
Blue veins raised under wrinkled skin,
the look of my mother about me.

I do the twist with a vacuum cleaner,
consult the dog about the grocery list,
smile fondly at women nursing babies.

Time slows when I rest against the windowsill
to watch a nuthatch collect sunflower seeds.
I fight the urge to dote on little boys at church.

Back when my hair was glossy and easy to toss,
the woman I've become would have been in my way.
I hold up the check-in line looking for my glasses.

An airport security agent scans my ID,
leans in close and whispers
No way do you look your age.

The saunter of youth returns.
I swing my carry-on off the belt
and remember how to fly.

slow day at the glass shop

Wet snow falls all day from a gray sky.
No customers.
I keep the store open, waiting,
and I sell one piece of Plexiglas.

No customers.
I reconcile the bank account.
I sell one piece of Plexiglas.
The bills stack up.

I reconcile the bank account.
Nothing new has been added,
but the bills stack up.
Business should improve next week.

Nothing new has been added,
although a few customers call.
Business should improve next week,
along with the weather.

Although a few customers call,
none of them place orders.
Along with the weather,
my ambition sags.

None of the callers place orders,
but they ask about our prices.
Wet snow falls from a gray sky.
I keep the store open, waiting.

harboring a mean streak

The patch of devil's club in my yard
lifts fiery spires of poison berries
on spiny stems above thorny leaves.

Vicious native plant. Touch it, you'll be sorry.
Even the berries have stickers.

Were I to dig it up, the soil would prove fertile.
Other shrubs with nicer traits could thrive there.
But what a chore, the roots are deep,
and I would miss that prickly wildness.

moose seasons

In the half light of a February mid-morning
a moose reduces my rugosa rose
to a few spiny stalks rooted in frozen ground.
Her methodical bite and chew, the way
her legs splay to hold her steady—
like me she's had enough of winter.

Moose know which foundations in our town
leak the most heat. They kneel before church,
bank, and senior center to crop April grass,
intent on a meal. Long-legged, one-ton animals
swinging dewlaps—hungry for spring.

The moose crossing our yard on a bright June night
has twins. Red-haired calves nose the swing set,
nurse and cavort as their skinny mother feeds.
She strips new leaves from a branch with one swipe.
I can't begrudge her the birch—
in four months she'll be pregnant again.

snowed in

Twenty inches and the storm persists.
Neighbors stuck in driveways, plowmen
overwhelmed. Town so quiet I hear
surf like a steady moan.

My house is a bright warm box
of books, candles, quilts.
One path to the woodshed,
another to the chicken coop.

Like a fairy-tale queen, I greet
a moose browsing on lilac twigs
just beyond window glass,
his antlers burdened with snow.

Have you ever rejoiced in uncertainty?
I've seen a storm turn into poetry.

tourist

1.

In Paris, svelte women swoop in and out of fashion houses
along the boulevard St. Germain where I hover
like a cliché, daring myself to claim an outdoor table.

The French waiter scoffs
when I order café au lait.
"Olé, olé," he sneers. "Espagnol?"

2.

Ravens fly low, sleek as Parisians in this white winter.
On new snow my skis swish like wings,
my uphill tracks point side to side like talons.

From the forest I catch the rude clack of raven talk.
I'm a stranger again, as foreign as when I clutched
a Michelin travel guide beneath *la Tour Eiffel*.

when i brought you home to mama

She sized you up, spread her hands,
circled toward the door as if to corral you.
She waved away the difference in our ages,
you being younger. She wanted me
to have your children.

Your hair, wild then, has thinned.
You've taken to wearing suspenders.
I remember you at Mesa Verde, sweet
under juniper shade, disappearing
with me among the vanished Anasazi.

The weight of marriage settled you.
Your brow grew stern. You traded
the pickup with loud exhaust pipes
for a family model, made room
between us for babies.

Husband, father, provident man.
Our grandson, a wisp in your arms,
inherits the blessing Mama saw in you.

coupled

Autumn calm lake,
white trunks, yellow leaves.

Inverted mountains, mirrored clarity.

We live so close I can't picture your face.
I know eyes, deep-set and earnest. Mouth,
a grin that tips higher on the left
when my right hand cups your cheek.

We were a secret crush, unlikely
to everyone but us. We dared to wed
our differences, melding through time
so that now I look at you to see myself.

You are my still water.

contemplating autumn

Green strength wilts down, blossoms spiral to seed.
Had nature taken its course with me I'd have no teeth.
The first cancer, or the second, would have spread;
my fibrillating heart might not have found a rhythm.

I'm the descendant of a straight-backed matriarchy.
My corseted ancestors succumbed young to influenza,
female maladies. Outstripping inheritance, I climb a hill
to read my future in the mountain view.

Ten good years, maybe more. Not knowing
about tomorrow, I enter a field of fireweed,
autumn's final flower blooming hot pink,
profuse, as if to express my desire: More fire.

acknowledgments

Thanks to the following journals in which these poems first appeared:

Bloodroot Literary Magazine: "Watching Mama's Figure,"
   "Mythology"
Cirque: "Building a Boat"
Cossack Review: "Boy, Still Visible"
Hawaii Pacific Review: "Acting My Age" published as
   "What Is Happening Here?"
Hobble Creek Review: "Uppity," "Visiting the Cemetery
   in Plains, Montana"
Rock and Sling: "A Young Child," "Widowmaker"
Ruminate: "September Clouds" published as "The Feather"

My thanks to James Engelhardt for inspired editing, to many teachers and mentors for their generosity, and to a group of poets—Debi, Mercedes, Bill, Ela, Erin, Nancy, and Nan—for being dear companions.

Note: The phrase "a sumptuous destitution" is from Emily Dickinson.